What Does She Want . . . and Where Can I Get It?

by

Ang

Illustrated by Michael R. McCord
www.mrmillustrations.com
E-mail: m-mccord2@comcast.net

Note for Librarians: A cataloguing record for this book is available from Library and Archives Canada at www.collectionscanada.ca/amicus/index-e.html
ISBN 1-4120-6949-1

Printed on paper with minimum 30% recycled fibre. Trafford's print shop runs on "green energy" from solar, wind and other environmentally-friendly power sources.

TRAFFORD
PUBLISHING™

Offices in Canada, USA, Ireland and UK

This book was published *on-demand* in cooperation with Trafford Publishing. On-demand publishing is a unique process and service of making a book available for retail sale to the public taking advantage of on-demand manufacturing and Internet marketing. On-demand publishing includes promotions, retail sales, manufacturing, order fulfilment, accounting and collecting royalties on behalf of the author.

Book sales for North America and international:
Trafford Publishing, 6E–2333 Government St.,
Victoria, BC V8T 4P4 CANADA
phone 250 383 6864 (toll-free 1 888 232 4444)
fax 250 383 6804; email to orders@trafford.com
Book sales in Europe:
Trafford Publishing (UK) Limited, 9 Park End Street, 2nd Floor
Oxford, UK OX1 1HH UNITED KINGDOM
phone 44 (0)1865 722 113 (local rate 0845 230 9601)
facsimile 44 (0)1865 722 868; info.uk@trafford.com
Order online at:
trafford.com/05-1860

10 9 8 7 6 5 4 3 2

Contents

From the Author

This book, *What Does She Want . . . and Where Can I Get It?,* is based on thousands of hours of conversations I have had with women.

For over 40 years I have worked in the beauty industry. Instead of standing around the "water cooler," I have stood "around the chair" listening to women talk about the men in their lives. This opportunity has allowed me an amazing view of what a woman really wants in a relationship with a man.

I don't have a degree in human relations, psychology, or an educational background to validate research results; however, I have found that listening to these women, combined with my own "in the trenches" dating history, has given me information I can share to offer great insight for men to solve the age-old mystery of "What does she want?"

This book is designed in a simple format that can be used as a reference guide designed primarily for the single and single again *man who desires a fabulous woman in his life!*

home.comcast.net/~angebooks/

Introduction

It is "Magic Time." *She* is on your mind every minute. Your concentration is limited and you can't think about anyone or anything else. When you are with her she makes you feel wonderful! In your heart you believe she is the "perfect" woman! Yes, you are smitten.

Many people refer to this feeling as infatuation. It is a state of mind that everyone has experienced. It is euphoric. It drives us to think silly, romantic thoughts. Poets and writers have written books, plays and songs about this wondrous thing we call "love."

In this state of unreasonable happiness we laugh for no apparent reason. It is virtually impossible for us to become angry, and we even lose our appetite! The outside world looks at us with a knowing smile remembering when "it" had happened to them!

In an ideal world we would live in "Magic Time" forever. However, we could not survive the ecstasy of this wondrous feeling for an extended time because we would drop dead from the adrenaline!

Reality approaches and now you find yourself on "Planet Nowhere." It is like being by yourself in the desert. For some unknown reason *she* won't go out with you, talk to you or even give you the time of day. Every man has lived on "Planet Nowhere." It is not a happy place.

Women love men and want to be desired by them. The truth is that men unknowingly "shoot themselves in the foot" when it comes to enticing and romancing a woman. He often shrugs, seems completely baffled and asks himself, "What does she want?"

This book is your secret toolbox for being successful with a woman. When you are emotionally healthy and understand the principles of making a woman happy, you can have a "once in a lifetime partnership." Follow me, and you can live in "Magic Time" and make "Planet Nowhere" disappear!

Chapter 1

The Dating Dance

“I like you. Do you like me?”

1

The Dating Dance

"I like you. Do you like me?"

The "dating dance" is the first step in the dating process. The man and the woman each determines if the other will be a candidate for dating. Casual dating (Level I) can vary in time from a few days to months. In some cases it never goes past the first date! The longer this dating phase continues, the better the couple will get to know one another. Many people in hindsight say they wished they had taken more time in casual dating before they had committed to an exclusive dating relationship.

Realistically this step is such a varied personal experience that there are no hard and fast rules. The first consideration in seeking a mate is deciding if there is a mutual "chemistry." This "it" factor is an indefinable combination of physical attraction and natural "comfort" level. After the initial meeting, and if a connection is established, subsequent dates will be planned. Are you, as they say, "into one another"?

In the animal world, the male often carries the bright colors or plumage and he uses these to entice and attract the female. One of the most visible examples of "showing" is evident by the colors on a male peacock. The feathers of the female of the species are gray in color, and it is the male that struts and flares his beautifully colored feathers to impress the female. It's as if he is saying, "Pick me!"

In the human world the reverse is usually true. The female uses her non-verbal communication skills to attract a male's attention. Non-verbal cues include her physical appearance and her demeanor. She will dress to impress and utilize her body language to let him "know" if she is interested in him. This is often the time you will hear a man say, "She knocked me off my feet!" or "It was love at first sight!" or "She had me at 'Hello.'" The female often accepts the role of the "huntee" and the male takes the counter role of the "hunter." How does the male attract the female? Within minutes of meeting the male, the female decides if he will be a possible mate. Her decision is based on his appearance, clothing and his demeanor (body language). It is very important that the male look his personal best. Communication is 90% body language and 10% spoken language. Your body speaks loudly and clearly long before a single word is uttered. You will never get another chance to create that all-important *first impression* again!

A man and woman often experience a *first date* by meeting for coffee or drink at a local restaurant. In some situations women prefer to pay for their refreshment so they will not feel obligated in any way. There is not a steadfast rule that dictates who pays the bill; however, the *gold standard* is the person who pays for the date is the one who extended the invitation. In today's "dating society" it is not uncommon for the female to invite the male to go to dinner or escort her to an event. Men are usually flattered by this gesture, but some are more comfortable seeking the date, at least in the beginning of the courtship. If the dating continues into an "exclusive" dating relationship (Level II), there tends to be more sharing of the planning and costs of entertainment and food.

An exclusive dating relationship is an agreement in which both agree to date only one another (Level II). This arrangement allows the couple to spend much more time together. During this time frame, which can be a few months to a year, the couple will learn more about the thoughts, dreams and habits of one another. Often this time is referred to as the "honeymoon" time of dating. Although not the usual, many couples will become engaged to be married during this period of dating. Exclusive dating announces to the world that you are publicly proclaiming you are now "a couple."

Courting is not confined to just the beginning of the dating dance. Women want and desire men to "court" them forever. Yes, I know, but it's in your best interest! In courting a woman, a man shows that he honors, respects and desires the female. Courting involves an effort that includes, but is not limited to, giving her flowers, a card, a compliment, an unexpected phone call, a small candy selection, a book, a music compact disc, or any number of thoughtful items that say in essence, "I am thinking of you." In fact, just "listening" to her and asking questions is a great start in letting a woman *know* that you are truly interested in her.

Dating does not have to be an expensive venture. Creativity can be really beneficial. Plan a number of "date" options. Some options might include a walk in a scenic location, a flea-market visit, a picnic (pick up food from a market), tennis, golf, running, a workout date at your gym, a free concert in the park, cooking dinner for her, inviting her to a party/dinner at a friend's house, a visit to a bookstore together and/or lunch at a local café.

When you spend time with a possible long-term partner, some of the characteristics you will be looking for include: a value system similar to your own, a healthy lifestyle, a sense of humor, financial stability, good family involvement, a balanced emotional and mental outlook, honesty, intelligence, and the ability and desire to commit to a relationship.

Some people joke that a man often spends more time selecting a car than a mate! Unfortunately, this can be true in some cases. It takes time and attention to achieve true intimacy and the excitement of having a fabulous partner in life. Finding a woman who will adore, honor, and always be there for you is worth all the effort, money and time you can expend. She is a "jewel" who will glorify your life!

Chapter 2

Relationship: Where Are You?

2

Relationship: Where Are You?

A woman desires to feel cherished, respected, and viewed as an equal partner. She wants to tell her friends and family, "He is so good to me." The following guide defines what a woman seeks in the three stages of a relationship.

Level I: Casual Dating Relationship

This first level is a *casual* dating time and is the first step in spending time together and getting to know the other person. Level I can be as short as one date or as long as six months!

Touching is minimal (a light kiss, a hug or holding hands).

Give her compliments (be sincere): "You look great!" "You have a wonderful smile!" "You have beautiful hair."

Call her on the phone 1-2 times per week. This will let you know that you are interested and still in the running. Phone calls are important!

Show interest in her activities (ask questions): "How was your day?"

Ask about family members or possible appointments she has mentioned.

Ask for a date 3-4 days in advance and call to confirm the date 24 hours in advance. I know this can be tedious, but it is necessary!

Send or bring a card or flower(s) or some other small gift, if inspired.

Offer to do minor household repairs, cook dinner, or be of some help by offering to do an errand. (It is called effort, and women love it.)

Show gentlemanly behavior (your best "charming self").

Level II: Exclusive Dating Relationship

At this level you have agreed to see one another exclusively. This is the direction taken when both of you anticipate a *long-term commitment*. (This is getting pretty serious!)

Be supportive and speak to her in positive affirmations: "You are wonderful!" "You handled that situation well." "You have beauty and brains!"

Be conscious of her moods and address them. (Show concern.)

Plan an event together, such as going to a play, concert, or perhaps a movie.

Call her on the phone several times a week (talk naughty!): "I miss your kisses!" "I can't wait to see you tonight!"

Be a proactive communicator (talk back and forth like a tennis game).

Create intimacy by offering her a neck or foot massage (oh, yes!).

Plan a private time such as a weekend trip out of town.

Surprise her with a small gift that you know she will like.

Offer to run errands, do some housekeeping, or help with a major household/car repair. (Ask, "What can I do for you?")

Work on a project with her. (Select something you *both* would like to do.)

Verbalize your commitment to the relationship: "We make a wonderful couple." "You have my heart." "I am so lucky to have you in my life!"

Be affectionate with her. Kiss her on the neck when she's not expecting it. Dance with her to the radio in the kitchen! Give her a big hug when you see her. Kiss her with much dramatic flair! (Think of the old romantic movie characters.)

Tease and joke with her. Come up with some inside jokes that only the two of you know about.

Level III: Committed or Married Relationship

The committed/married relationship is a serious partnership and is an agreement to be a "couple" in all ways. This relationship is a total commitment and is meant to last a lifetime!

Be her best friend. (Be an ally.)

Use positive support words concerning her interests: "How is the project going?" "Your opinion is important to me."

Call her often (sometimes to just "check in").

Give her a total evening of intimacy based on *her* desires. Ask her what she wants. Plan a spontaneous weekend away or plan a party to entertain mutual friends. Don't be a guest: Be the "host"!

Surprise her by washing her car or finishing a small project without her expecting it. (Big points for this one!)

Plan a vacation together, away from friends and family (romantic and fun, please).

Have a weekly date night for just the two of you. (Go somewhere different each week.)

Surprise her with a romantic dinner at home without children or family members!

Gifts are appropriate and expected. (Send flowers "for no reason"!)

Tell her how you feel about her: "I love you." "I adore you." "I am such a lucky man!"

Chapter 3

Talk To Me Baby!

Words Are So Sexy!

3

Talk To Me Baby!
Words Are So Sexy!

It is well known that women are very word driven. We have thousands of more words a day to say than a man might speak in a week. Women accuse men of withholding important information just by not talking to us about everything! Of course, the guys seem to be overwhelmed by the thought of creating so much talking over what they see as "trivial" conversation. So it goes. We want words and you guys want silence.

Compromise makes the world go around, so I have designed a list of phrases any man can memorize, and when prodded, he can make the female happy by saying these words. A woman commented, "I only want him to say the words if he is really sincere." Trust me, gentlemen, when you see the results from this new vocabulary, you will learn to be sincere as well as ecstatic, because she will respond to the words like a duck to water. The phrases can be interchanged, so select the ones you like and repeat them often.

The thing to remember is "pick your battles." No sane man wants to fight with the woman in his life. Practice saying these phrases, and remember that using them will save your life and make her happy!

"Honey, whatever makes you happy makes me happy!"

"What can I do for you?"

"Yes, dear."

"Thank you."

"Please."

"I am sorry."

"You are wonderful."

"Honey, don't worry about it. I will take care of it."

"How was your day?"

"You are so beautiful!"

"I love you."

"I can see you are upset. Do you want to talk about it?"

"You always look great to me."

Chapter 4

Romance: Off to Planet Romance

4

Romance: Off To Planet Romance

Romance: To make love or woo: to seek favor of, to court as by flattery, gifts.
(Merriam-Webster Online Dictionary)

Women want to feel excitement, anticipation, desire, closeness, and intimacy when they think of romance. Romance can be present at every level of a relationship; however, in a casual dating relationship, true intimacy is not appropriate. Here are the four (4) cornerstones to creating *romance* in a committed relationship.

I. Words

Words can stimulate a woman as much as a physical touch. Women respond strongly to "sweet nothings" equally well as they do to being stroked, held, or being made love to.

1. Tell her how she makes you feel. Examples: "You make me want to be a better man." "I am so proud when you are with me!"

2. Whisper to her: "You smell wonderful!" "I want to kiss you."

3. Tell her how desirable/beautiful she is to you.

4. Whisper those "sweet nothings" in her ear, such as "I am crazy about you!" "You are wonderful!" "What can I do for you?" "I am a lucky man to have you!" "What a woman!" "What would I do without you?" "Come closer to me so I can feel your body." "Let's pretend we are on a secluded beach and are lying on our backs looking at the stars." "I never want to let you go."

5. Say something that will make her laugh (this is very sexy!)

II. Actions

Your actions truly do speak louder than words. Sending or bringing flowers is only *one* of many romantic gestures!

1. Mail her a card with a personal note. "I miss you." "You are wonderful!" "I am excited about seeing you again."

2. Search for her in a crowd, seek direct eye contact and smile.

3. Move your lips silently and say, "I love you," or "Come here."

4. Write a personal note (a little naughty can be exciting) and leave it somewhere for her to find (sticky notes are great!)

5. Touch her arm or her back to acknowledge her presence.

6. Gently brush the hair out of her eyes or back from her face.

7. Flirt with her. (Wink and send a silent kiss.)

8. Give her a hug or reach down and hold her hand.

9. Give her a little kiss (on the neck, hand or cheek).

10. Kiss her gently at first and then deepen the kiss gradually.

11. Surprise her with a small gift or flowers.

III. Physical Intimacy

Intimacy is more than sex; it is the *way you approach* her physically.

1. Look directly into her eyes before kissing her.

2. Give her total one-on-one attention.

3. Lightly kiss her lips before kissing her more deeply. (Sloppy kisses are a big turn-off!)

4. Use your hands to touch her face (cup her face in your palms with her chin resting on the base of your hands) and kiss her gently.

5. Lightly kiss her neck or ear, or one of the key erogenous zones.

6. Caress her shoulders (softly rub).

7. When in bed, spoon her body (cuddle up).

8. Take her hand, turn it over, and look at her as you kiss the palm. (Wow!)

9. Massage her body slowly and easily. (Begin at the feet, ankles and move upward towards the top of her body and then end with a head massage.)

10. Cover her face with small "butterfly" kisses.

11. Whisper to her when you are physically close (a little naughty is good).

12. Give lots of foreplay (we don't mean football).

13. It is absolutely imperative that you are *squeaky clean* and *smelling fresh* to have intimate moments with a woman. The smell of tobacco, alcohol, body odor or any hint of bad breath will ruin the moment.

IV. Body Language

Possessiveness is not romantic! She needs to feel desired, not owned. Show her you care by being gentle and caring.

1. Lean forward to speak to her.

2. Give her a "wink" to share a joke or thought.

3. Stay close to her physically (approximately 18 inches or closer).

4. Lean your entire body into hers for a caress (full body contact).

5. Nuzzle her on the neck.

6. Walk up behind her and run your hands down the sides of her body.

7. Dance with her in the house!

8. Sing to her if you have a good voice.

9. Give her a big smile when she comes into the room. (White clean teeth are a major turn-on!)

10. Stand up and give her direct eye contact.

Chapter 5

Special Occasions: Don't Forget!

5

Special Occasions: Don't Forget!

Any special occasion or holiday is a time of celebration. The following is a guide to making her special occasion a memorable one.

Note: Never give the woman in your life a gift that has a cord or a plug unless she specifically has requested it!

VALENTINE'S DAY

This special occasion is the most romantic time of the year!

Remember and mark your calendar for February 14!

Give her a card with a written personal note: "I am crazy about you!"

Hand her a single flower. (We love this gesture!)

Present or send flowers (in her favorite color).

If purchasing chocolate in a box, make sure it is in a heart-shaped box.

Select four pieces of her favorite gourmet chocolate and have them wrapped!

Purchase a personal gift such as jewelry or lingerie (something she wouldn't buy herself).

Plan dinner at a nice restaurant (and make reservations a minimum of two weeks in advance).

Make plans for child care. (Yes, you can call a babysitter!)

THANKSGIVING

This special occasion can be highly family focused. Here are a few observations.

Accept her invitation or ask her to join you for the day.

As a guest, you should take flowers, chocolate or wine to the host.

Participate in the day's activities and be sure to include her.

CHRISTMAS
Look/Listen/Learn

Beginning in October, start watching her movements and listen to what she says for "gift ideas." Quiz her best friend/sister/mother about helping you to select the best Christmas gift for her. Only buy clothing for her if she trusts your fashion sense!

Present her with a Christmas card with a personally written note. Examples: "Thank you for just being you." "Honey it's been a wonderful year with you!"

Giving her a small gift on Christmas Eve will start a tradition that she will love you for. (This time is the perfect one to present her with a piece of jewelry.)

Surprise her by giving her a gift she would not buy for herself.

Money should only be given if she absolutely needs it. If giving money/gift card or gift certificate, always include a small material gift also.

BIRTHDAY

This day is *her* day and is the most important day of the year for her.

Mark her birthday date on your calendar!

Write a personal note inside a nice birthday card.

Buy her favorite cake or, better yet, bake it yourself!

Offer to take her shopping and buy her a new outfit!

Ask her, ahead of time, what she wants to do or what gift she would like.

Take a day off from work/business on her birthday and spend the day with her.

Give her something she would not buy for herself.

Invite her to a weekend or overnight hotel stay (you make all of the plans).

Take her out to dinner at a nice restaurant (make reservations if necessary).

ANNIVERSARY

This is the time she truly wants to spend with you. You should make it a time of remembrance, when you met, how you met, and what the two of you have done in your relationship since the last anniversary.

Mark your calendar!

Give her card with a very personal note/letter inside telling her what she means to you. Examples: "You make my life wonderful!" "You are the best!"

Start a tradition by purchasing her a piece of jewelry or a collectible.

Take a day off from work and spend it with her!

Ask her ahead of time what she wants to do or what gift she wants.

Take her out to dinner at a nice restaurant (make reservations if necessary).

Plan a special trip for the both of you (surprise her).

MOTHER'S DAY

This day is important to everyone. However, *all* mothers should be acknowledged on this day!

If you have children, help them plan a "special" day for Mom.

If your mother or mother figure is alive, make an effort to send her a card or flowers.

If you are married, acknowledge your wife's mother as well as your own.

If you are dating a woman and there is an absentee father, then offer to take the the children shopping for their mother.

Chapter 6

Clothing: You Are What You Wear!

6

Clothing: You Are What You Wear!

Building a wardrobe is simply the process of putting together basic clothing pieces that may be used interchangeably to create a number of versatile outfits. A man's wardrobe is important and says a lot about who he is. The way you dress creates a lasting impression on everyone you meet. Below is the list of clothing items a man should own categorized into five (5) groups.

Dress/business wear
Casual/date/social
Athletic/work out/physical work
Outerwear/coats and jackets/underwear
Home wear

Rules

1. Buy the best you can afford!

2. Are you clothing challenged? Ask a friend that has a great sense of style to shop with you.

3. If you haven't worn it in a year, then donate it, sell it, toss it, or pack it away in a box for the relatives to throw away after you die.

LEVEL I: "Mr. Good Body"
Every man needs this basic wardrobe.

Dress/business wear:

1 suit (navy or dark in color) and 1 sport coat/blazer (navy or black),

both made of year-round fabric. Add 2 pairs of nice dress pants to go with the blazer either in a gray or a deep khaki color. Purchase six (6) dress shirts (long sleeve), 3 white, 2 blue and 1 in a pale or tone-on-tone colored fabric. The shirt fabric needs to be of good quality cotton.

Purchase 2 ties, 1 in a red color and the other in a soft blue or gray print. Dress shoes should be either black or cordovan in color, a lace-up style with thin soles. Dark socks are recommended for dress wear (6 pairs). Match socks with your trouser color. A belt in either dark brown, cordovan or black completes the look. Your belt and shoes should be in the same color family. In selecting a suit consider that a single-breasted jacket with 3 buttons will have the most slenderizing appearance.

Casual/date/social:

You will need a total of 4 pairs of casual slacks. Select 2 pairs in khaki colors (1 pair light colored and 1 pair dark in tone), 1 pair in a gray color and 1 pair in a dark color (navy, black or brown).

Include 2 pairs of jeans to be worn for social situations (dress jeans that have been purchased within 2 years). Long sleeved dress shirts may be used in casual wear. The balance of the shirt wardrobe should include short and long sleeved polo shirts. Select various colors and patterns to your taste, although it is always safe to select a solid color in white, red or blue. A polo shirt looks great under a sport coat for most casual situations. Socks should be of a cotton/wool blend and match your trouser color. You will need 3 sweaters in light to medium weight (cotton preferred): 1 in white or off-white, 1 in a bright color, and one 1 in a navy or black. Shoes for casual wear include: loafers or similar shoe style, and even occasionally a nice leather sandal. In the south it is not unusual to wear shorts with a shirt for casual wear because of the warm climate. Keep 3 pairs of shorts for casual wear in khaki or neutral colors. The shorts should be cut well (not too baggy or too tight) and have loops to accommodate a belt. The best choice in length should be 2-4 inches above the knee.

Athletic/workout/physical wear:

You will need a minimum of 6 short sleeve t-shirts in good condition. Add 3 or more pairs of cotton/nylon shorts, 2-3 pairs of sweat pants, sweatshirts and a good pair of athletic cross-training shoes. Add 6 pairs of thick white athletic socks and a good pair of sandals with rubber and/or nylon straps. One good bathing suit should be included in your wardrobe. Select one that is cut to flatter your body type. A shirt that compliments the swimsuit can make you appear well-dressed. Don't forget to purchase an athletic set, which includes a jacket and pants that are coordinated or sold together. Women do look at men in athletic wear. Do not dress sloppy.

Outerwear/coats and jacket/underwear:

One lightweight wool or microfiber medium length coat, one short light weight wind breaker (nice quality) and 1 all-weather coat. You will need one pair of good leather gloves. In underwear select boxers or jockey briefs (6 or more pairs) and good quality underwear t-shirts (6 or more). All underwear should be replaced once a year.

Home wear:

This clothing is what you wear around your home. You will need 4 t-shirts in good condition, 2 pairs of casual jeans, 2 pairs of sweatpants, 2 sweatshirts, 1-2 pairs of sleep pants and, 1 pair of worn (but presentable) athletic shoes.

All remaining clothing should be placed into 3 categories:

1. Memory clothing (old clothing you have an emotional attachment to but don't wear any more.) You know, those t-shirts, sweatshirts or even dress shirts that were your favorites. Place this clothing in a box, label and place on the top shelf of your closet.

2. Clothing that is in good condition that you never wear. You just don't

really like it or it does not fit you. Pack this clothing and donate to a charity, sell it or give to a friend or a relative.

3. All remaining clothing that is stained or is in need of major repair needs to be thrown out!

LEVEL II: "Mr. Up and Coming"
Basic + Upgrade to a professional wardrobe

You own the basic wardrobe and now you want to upgrade it and include more professional clothing. Level II includes more suits, shirts and a few luxury items. In your closet you will need 2 additional suits in varying but subtle patterns in neutral color palettes such as gray, black, navy and tan. These suits should be in a 100% worsted wool tropical weight. You need at least 2 more sport coats above the basic wardrobe (Level I), and it is recommended you select one in a soft texture and perhaps one in a neutral weave. Wearing a sport coat and slacks isn't usually considered "dressing up." However, most gentlemen wear them to casual events and parties, and it is standard wear for most offices or job positions. For the Level II wardrobe you will want to upgrade the quality of your shirts by selecting 100% pinpoint cotton construction as well as "better" quality sports shirts and slacks.

In purchasing sweaters, select one or two with a handmade quality and, if possible, add a cashmere sweater. Shoes are investment items so buy well-made shoes for dress wear and soft Italian leather for casual wear. Select ties that are unique and different, but not garish or too bright in color. People will remember you and your beautiful ties. It is better to have 6 great ties than 12 okay ties!

Overall, the Level II wardrobe has not only more but better quality items than the basic. A good leather "bomber" jacket or blazer can be a nice addition to your clothing wardrobe. If you play golf or tennis, you should purchase excellent athletic wear. You will be competing with other business people and it pays to look good when networking. This is when you are what you wear!

LEVEL III: "Mr. Big Shot"

The best of the best in clothing

You are known as "the best-dressed man." At this level you will want to trade with the finest men's clothing establishments available. Maintain a relationship with one or two top-notch sales people that will keep you "in the know" about fabrics and design selections suited just for you. You own the best quality suits that are available and they are often custom made. Some of the designer names in your closet will include Armani, Prada and Burberry. Accessories include fine leather, alligator and other exotic skins in belts, shoes and wallets. At this level of dressing it is customary to have custom-made shirts that are monogrammed. Sweaters are made of cashmere and silk. You own a custom made-to-fit tuxedo.

Review and Update

Professional clothing experts recommend that you go through and organize your clothes once a year. It is important that you have a full-length mirror available to check the fit of your clothing. One of the best investments you can make is using a talented tailor/seamstress. They can make you appear 10 years younger and up to 10 pounds lighter just by fitting your clothes correctly.

ACCESSORIES

Jewelry

A well-dressed man wears no more than 4 pieces of jewelry at one time. Including a watch, you may also select a pair of cuff links, bracelet, ring or similar combination. Remember the maximum number is four.

A. Watches: A metal watch, either stainless steel or gold tone, works well for dress and professional wear. Leather band watches work best for casual/professional wear. When active in athletics wear a sport watch.

B. Necklaces: Other than wearing a chain with a religious symbol it is best not to wear much in the form of a necklace. Men with careers in the theater, music and the arts and entertainment set different standards for themselves, and it is certainly up to the situation and the taste of the gentleman.

D. Rings: A wedding ring, initial ring or any another ring of good quality is attractive. After 5 years it is time to put the college ring away as a keepsake.

E. Earrings: These are more a fashion statement and have little to do with any investment purchase in a wardrobe.

Eyeglasses

Glasses should be chosen that flatter the man's facial shape and should be updated every 3-5 years. Replace broken frames immediately. Allow a professional or a friend to assist you in the selection of a new set of frames. Old pairs of glasses can be donated at the optical stores.

Leather Goods

Fine leather accessories, such as wallets, shoes and belts, complete the well-dressed man's wardrobe. Women are quick to notice quality accessories. In the line of belts, the one-inch wide belt is reserved for dress wear. Wider belts are the best choice to be used with casual wear.

Underwear

A man needs 6 or more sets of underwear. A set includes an undershirt and a pair of boxers or briefs. Once a year all underwear needs to be replaced.

Boxer briefs should be worn if you are slender to average in weight. Regular boxers are a better selection if you are large in the middle of your body.

Briefs are to be used under dress pants that are thin in material and whenever support is needed. Bikinis and thongs are best used for intimate moments and *only* if your lady likes them.

Questions and Answers

1. *Why is it important to dress well?*

   Body language is 90% of communication. People (rightly or wrongly) *do* form an opinion of you just by the way you are dressed.

2. *I do not have the money to buy all new clothes. What do I do?*

   The clothing guide is simply a suggested list of what you need in your wardrobe. The main thing to remember is to "buy the best clothing you can afford." Investment clothing is a term used in purchasing a piece of clothing that will wear well. You will be able to wear it over and over again and still look good. It is smarter to buy better quality than to buy poor quality items. Discard clothing that is not appropriate or of poor quality, but keep the better quality items that you will wear many times. When you are able financially, purchase additional pieces necessary to finish your wardrobe.

3. *Tell me why having a really nice set of clothing will profit me.*

   Dressing well gives you confidence and actually causes you to stand up straighter in posture.

   Women are very impressed with a man who pays attention to his appearance, and they form an opinion within 2 minutes of meeting.

   In seeking employment or a position with a company, the best-dressed applicants are favored.

   Dressing well can enhance your best features and help you appear to your best advantage.

Chapter 7

Flowers, Flowers: A Pocket Full of Posies

7

Flowers, Flowers: A Pocket Full of Posies

To give or not to give is the question!
Flowers are always welcomed by a woman.
You just need to know *when* and *what* to give her!

When Do You Give Flowers to a Woman?

Women love flowers for "special occasions" and "for no reason at all." Special occasions include the following.

Valentine's Day: This is the most romantic holiday of the year.

Birthday (her special day): You miss this day and you are a goner!

A promotion, recognition time, or even the first day at a new job: Applaud her by sending flowers.

New baby (everyone is happy): Send flowers to the mother, not the baby.

Anniversary: A celebration to be remembered.

Mother's Day: (your mother and her mother).

No reason: Sending flowers "for no reason at all" is a highly romantic gesture. The element of surprise will earn you big points, especially with a "thinking of you" card attached.

I am sorry: Make these flowers a very elaborate offering and do not forget to include a card with a sincere written apology.

Where Do You Find Flowers?

Flowers can be found everywhere: at your local florist, the supermarket, a roadside vendor, and even on the Internet. The key is to purchase the best you can afford that suits the occasion, even if it is for "no reason at all." Ask the woman what her favorite color or flower is. Order flowers based upon her answers and you will be "the man."

Why Should You Use a Local Florist?

Top-flight florists keep a record of all occasion-giving dates and will send you a reminder to send flowers.

They will educate you on what flowers to send her and will make you look good.

It is quick and efficient. You can pick up the phone and place an order for flowers in a flash. (Yes, it can be easy!)

Roses

Florists know that a majority of women prefer *colored roses* rather than the traditional red roses. Send her roses (1 dozen please, minimum) in her favorite color, yellow, coral, pink or one of the mixed hybrid colors.

Best Selections

A florist-recommended bouquet with the freshest flowers available in a vase delivered to her home or business.

A dozen roses delivered (two dozen roses, if you have money or you have been really bad).

Orchids, tulips, peonies or number of other exotic flowers that your florist recommends.

Worst Selections

Carnations, corsages (proms only), and no dried flower arrangements, please.

A green plant is not a flower.

Baskets of flowers are not romantic. Send flowers in vases.

Chapter 8

Manners: What Your Mama Taught You!

8

Manners: What Your Mama Taught You!

Using good manners is simply a way of showing courtesy and thoughtfulness. Women *notice* how a man treats them as well as how they conduct themselves around others. A gentleman always treats others with kindness.

General Manners

A woman considers it a courtesy for a man to offer to open a door or pull out a chair for her. Some women will accept this; others will want to do it themselves. The key is to offer!

When walking with a woman, you should walk beside her, not in front of her. If walking on the side of a street, walk between her and the traffic as a courtesy.

During conversation, maintain eye contact, listen to her viewpoint, and be an active participant (ask questions). It is like a tennis game going back and forth.

When you meet someone you know, be sure that you introduce your date/companion. If you do not remember the name of the acquaintance, introduce your date/mate first.

If you must cancel a date, do it for the right reasons: illness, business emergency, or personal emergency. It is a courtesy to offer to call to reschedule the broken date.

Table Manners

Table manners can impress your date or partner, but not using manners can sabotage the relationship. The following actions should be *avoided* at all costs.

Putting too much food in your mouth at one time (gross).

Talking with food in your mouth (double-gross).

Using your utensils like tools ("shoveling").

Elbows and arms on table while eating (guarding your food).

Tucking a napkin around your neckline (only when eating lobster).

Wearing a hat inside the building, much less at the table.

Drinking too much. (This is embarrassing for everyone.)

Flirting with a female wait staff member.
(Women really hate this one!)

Pointers to Remember During a Meal

Be kind and considerate to service personnel.

Place your napkin in your lap and use it.

Maintain eye contact and focus on your dinner companion. (Smile.)

Let her take the lead when starting the meal. (Wait for her to start.)

Do not rush by eating too quickly. (It's not a race!)

Excuse yourself from the table for personal matters (such as blowing your nose or burping).

After the meal, before paying the bill, ask if she would like coffee, dessert, or an after-dinner drink.

Paying the Bill

Always assume you are paying the bill unless she has offered before the meal is served. She doesn't need to see the total or details.

Pick up the bill *promptly*, review charges *quickly*, and then pay.

Tip accordingly (15-20%).

Cell Phones

Use of these phones in a public area has become a national problem. If you must take a call, excuse yourself and walk out of the public area. Keep your voice down to avoid disturbing others who are in close proximity. You should turn off the phone ringer or place the ringer in a vibrate mode in public areas such as these.

Funerals	Churches
Sports Events	Doctors' Offices
Meetings	Hair Salons
Grocery Stores	Shopping Malls
Theaters	Weddings
Restaurants	

In a social situation turn the phone off and leave it in the car. She does not want to share your time together with *you* talking on the phone!

Chapter 9

Are You a Winner?

Take a Test.

9

Are You a Winner? Take a test.

A winner is a person who, on a consistent basis, does everything right! We know that winners have distinct qualities that allow them to be outstanding in many ways.

Check the list below to see how many *winner's* qualities you have.

Posture	Stands tall with confidence
Attitude	Views the world in a positive way
Appearance	Visually "put together" (smart looking)
Manners	Respectful of social graces (a gentleman)
Communicates	Speaks clearly and enunciates his words
Kind	Respectful of others
Financially Stable	Manages money well
Healthy	Maintains a "healthy" lifestyle
Courageous	Steps forward without fear
Resolute	Problem solver
Focused	Goal oriented
Balanced	Keeps work and family life balanced

Generous	Gives time and money
Intelligent	Thinks before he acts
Compassionate	Possesses empathy for the less fortunate
Decision Maker	Makes timely decisions
Self-Controlled	Emotionally level (no anger issues)
Good Humor	Appreciates and "sees" humor in life
Flexible	Adjusts to change
Good Loser	Graciously accepts defeat
Honorable	A man of his word

Scoring

1-5	You are on your way!
6-10	You are some woman's hero!
11-15	You are one in a million!

Chapter 10

First Impression: Make It a Good One!

10

First Impression: Make It a Good One!

A first impression cannot be changed. Within two minutes of meeting a woman, she will form an opinion of your desirability. She will be looking at the following.

Attitude is the total look of a winner!

Smile. (It makes us feel important.)

Make direct eye contact (meant for us)!

Be attentive, alert, and enthusiastic. (Look alive!)

Exhibit good posture by standing up straight with your shoulders held back. (Good posture makes you look taller.)

Look confident. (Be sure of yourself.)

If appropriate, offer a firm ("manly") handshake.

Physical appearance can make or break that first impression!

Strive to be height-and-weight proportionate (based on health charts).

Make sure you have a good haircut (a must).

Have clean and neatly trimmed nails.

A good complexion is very appealing. (Smooth is always good!)

Be freshly showered and shaved. (Oh, yes!)

Apply deodorant liberally.

Women love clean, white teeth. (White teeth are sexy!)

Lightly use aftershave or cologne balm. (We like you smelling good!)

If seated, sit erect (no slumping, please).

Keep you arms relaxed by your side.
(Crossed arms indicate a closed attitude.)

Clothing says much about who you are!

Clothing should be clean, pressed, and fitted properly.

Wear polished shoes or clean athletic sneakers.

Remove hats and caps while inside the building.

First Few Words: Don't Ruin It!

Introduce yourself and keep it simple.

Be genuine and authentic. (Women don't like "cute" remarks.)

Chapter 11

Dating: Everyone Is Doing It!

11

Dating: Everyone Is Doing It!

Date: A social engagement
between two persons that often
has a romantic character.
(Merriam-Webster Online Dictionary)

In the past "dating" was considered a process for young unmarried people. In today's society with our high divorce rates, late marriages, and widowhood, "dating" possibilities have opened up for people of all ages. Dating can be full of anxiety. Outlined is a guide that will help prepare you for this great adventure. Remember, no one is an expert at this, so take a deep breath and join the fun!

1. Be prepared.

2. Decide whom you would like to date. (Let's be realistic now!)

3. Ask yourself if she is available, approachable and interested in you. (Ask around if she is available and find out what you can about her.)

4. Look sharp! A woman knows within 2 minutes if you will be a candidate for dating. What is she considering? She is watching your body language, noting if your posture is good, that you are dressed well and have a smile on your face. It is a fact that body language is 90% and verbal language is only 10% in telling someone who you are. Create a good first impression. If in fact you will be speaking with her on the phone, use a strong voice, practice good English and allow her to *hear* who you are.

5. Transportation: Do you have a car that is clean and suitable to take a lady out on a date? The fact is most women, as a number one priority,

consider the cleanliness of your car long before they look at the make and model! Although trucks are technically transportation, they are not the best choice for dating! Women are not impressed.

Strategy

1. Will you ask her in person or on the telephone? It is easier for her to say no to you over the phone than in person.

2. Decide where you would like to take her and when. Make plan A, then make plan B, and then plan C. Have some alternatives just in case the original plan isn't going to work; remember, plan your strategy.

3. Select the best time to ask her out on a date. It's all about timing, so don't ask at a time she is frantically multitasking! Look for direct eye contact and a time when she is able to give you her total attention.

Approach

1. "Smile" as you approach her and say "hello." (Show those beautiful white teeth!) Women do not really like to have men try to be "cute" with them.

2. Introduce yourself (if you have not formally met before).

3. Open a conversation by asking her a question. Example: "How are you doing?" or "Can you believe this weather?"

4. Ask for the date. Examples: "I would like to take you to dinner this weekend. Would you be available?" "Would you have time for a cup of coffee?" "May I call you for a date?"

5. Exhibit good manners. (Be your charming self!)

Responding to her answer

Affirmative - *Yes*

1. Set up a specific time, location, and dress code, and offer her a phone number where you may be reached.

2. Ask her for a phone number where she may be reached.

3. Tell her you are looking forward to the date, and you will call and confirm the day before.

Negative - *No*

Do you think she is dating someone else, has a previous engagement, or is she just not interested? She may offer any of several reasons of why she will not go out with you. Respect what she says. However, if you are really interested, try for a second chance by offering these two choices to her.

1. Offer to reschedule the date at a more convenient time for her.

2. Offer your phone number on a card and tell her, "I would really like to take you out, so if your circumstances change, please call me."

If she does not accept either of the offers, accept her refusal, smile and be a gentleman as you leave.

Chapter 12

Kiss or Miss?

Give me a smooch, lover!

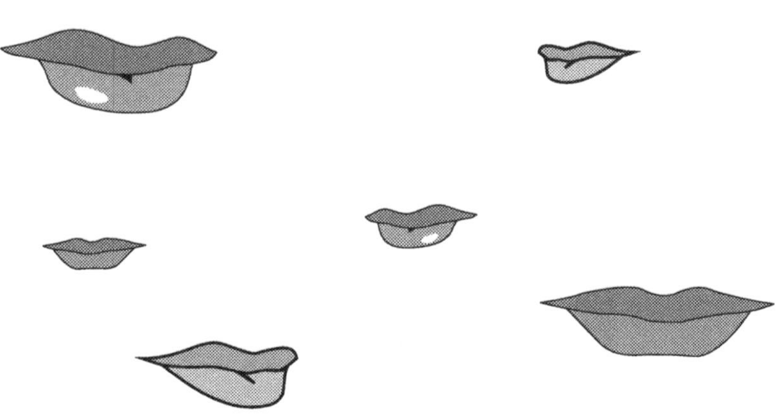

12

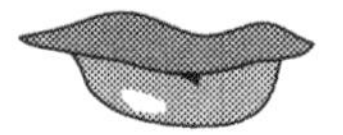

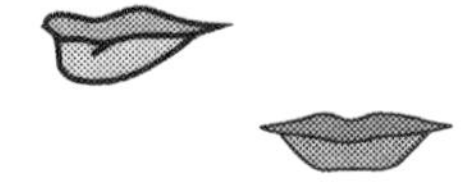

Kiss or Miss?

Give me a smooch, lover!

It has been said that a "great" kiss is like a great meal. Once you have experienced the best you never forget where it was and whom you were with!

A kiss is the key to the door of romance.

A badly executed kiss can "kill" a romantic interlude.

The longer a man waits before seeking the first kiss from a woman, the more interested she will become.

A woman will not kiss a man with bad breath or poor dental hygiene.

Look for permission to kiss a woman by looking into her eyes.

Kissing a woman on the neck "slow and easy" is a wonderful form of foreplay.

A woman loves a man who understands the dynamics of giving a great kiss.

How Do You Give a Great Kiss?

Check that your breath is clean and fresh. The beginning of the kiss should be gentle. Do not exert much pressure as you place your lips on hers. Lips should be just barely open and smooth to the touch. Allow the kiss to be slow, easy and deepen with time. Allow her to guide you on the intimacy of the kiss. Wait and let her end the kiss!

Kissing Techniques

The following kissing techniques used alone, or in combination, should be *avoided* at all costs. If you use them, they will send you directly to "Planet Nowhere"!

The Darter: This kisser opens his mouth and tends to dart his tongue back and forth quickly and deeply into the woman's mouth (like an anteater).

The Hole: This kisser opens his mouth very wide and presses his mouth over the entire mouth of the unsuspecting woman (like a huge empty well).

The Washer: This kisser uses his tongue to seek every area of the mouth, leaving a trail of saliva in his wake (like being drowned by wetness).

The Stiff Lip: This kisser has hard, flat unrelenting lips that do not move at all (like kissing a wall).

The Pucker: This kisser puckers up like a child and stands perfectly still, bent at the waist (no body contact). He pushes against the woman's lips (like kissing a piece of dried fruit).

The Biter: This kisser bites his way in and around her mouth. It forces the woman to withdraw to avoid being chewed to death (like being attacked by an animal).

Chapter 13

Grooming: Look Sharp!

13

Grooming: Look Sharp!

Groom: To make neat or attractive.
(Merriam-Webster Online Dictionary)

Cleanliness, from head to toe, is critical ! Women love their men clean and fresh! If you are single and dating, committed or married, it is always important to be clean and smelling fresh.

Hair: What to Do with It!

Every 4 weeks find the best stylist you can afford and get a *good* haircut. This does not mean stop by any shop/salon and let just any stranger cut your hair. Be selective about a stylist. Convenience is great but don't make it the first call.

Purchase recommended hair products and use them.

Closely trim nose, neck and ear hair and eyebrows weekly. There are small clippers you may purchase to help you maintain a neat appearance.

Excessive back, neck and ear hair should be controlled through shaving, waxing, trimming, or by laser hair removal administered by a dermatologist. You must be brave!

Shave daily or more often if warranted.

If you wear a mustache and/or a beard, keep them closely trimmed and neat.

If you want a more youthful appearance by using hair color,

make an appointment with a hair colorist specialist. Do not attempt this process yourself or you could end up looking like a bad Elvis!

Bald men can be sexy!

Hats do not cover up the fact you are balding.

Women realize 90% of the time that you are wearing a toupee, even if it is a good one.

Hair Styles to Avoid

Comb-over styles, toupees (really bad ones), and mullets. (Women hate these looks.)

Shaved head (only if you are mostly bald).

Black hair color (Elvis was the only one who could wear it).

High hair (sprayed within an inch of its life).

Gangster hair (slicked straight back from the face).

Helmet hair (combed flat across the top and sprayed stiff). This style tends to be the favorite look of some politicians.

Skin (Body): Protection/Prevention

Take short showers. (Too much hot water depletes the body of natural moisture.)

Use deodorant liberally after each shower/bath. You should use a roll-on deodorant rather than a spray. You will receive better protection from a roll-on, and the spray can stain your clothing, not to mention taking your breath away.

Visit a dermatologist annually for a full skin review. (Skin cancer is very serious.)

When in the sun, wear a cap or hat, sunglasses, and sun block (30 SPF or higher) on your face, including your lips and ears.

Face: Cleanse, Treat, Moisturize, and Protect

Seek a professional skin care specialist (at department stores, spas, or at a physician's office). Purchase and use recommended products to maintain great skin.

Clean your face once or twice daily with a pH-balanced cleansing bar. This product removes dirt from the face without removing the natural moisture content. A deodorant bar used in the shower is not a good choice to use on your face.

Treat your face twice a week with an Alpha Hydroxy (AHA) or a lactic acid product to remove dead skin. These products promote the removal of debris from the face and stimulate new cell growth. They are readily available in drug stores, skin care stores, and physicians' offices.

Moisturize: Apply a light moisturizer after shaving and just before using a *small amount* of shaving balm or lotion. If needed, use a more intense moisturizer around the eye area.

Protect: Apply a sunscreen product with an SPF of 30 or higher to the face, neck, and ear area. Do not forget to apply a similar product to your lips.

When using an aftershave balm or lotion, apply with a light touch; a heavy fragrance is not well received.

Nails: Clean and Trimmed

Cut short (straight across).

If nails are professionally manicured, have your nails buffed (not polished).

Keep fingernail cuticles neat by gently pushing back the cuticles with a washcloth during a shower or bath.

Apply a hand cream twice a day (available without fragrance).

Avoid biting your nails!

Feet: Trimmed Nails and Smooth Skin

Toenails cut (straight across).

Old skin exfoliated (use recommended product).

Calluses scrubbed down, softened, and moisturizer applied.

Teeth: Brush and Floss

Brush your teeth twice a day (helps eliminates bad breath).

When brushing your teeth remember to brush your tongue.

Use a mouthwash regularly (twice a day).

Floss your teeth thoroughly twice a day. (Gum disease can cause the loss of teeth.)

Have your teeth professionally cleaned twice a year.

Have all recommended dental repair work done.

Lighten/whiten your teeth for a more youthful appearance (sexy).

Bad breath will ruin your social life, but it is also a sign of dental problems.

Cosmetic dentistry is available to everyone, and you, too, can have a beautiful smile!

Keep breath mints handy. (Anticipate kissing.)

Chapter 14

Damage Control: In the Doghouse

14

Damage Control: In the Doghouse

She is not speaking to you and you have no idea why. You have been sent to Planet Nowhere! Nothing will change until you find out the cause. No, gentlemen, it will not blow over or go away. Select a "quiet" place to talk with no interference. Yes, this means turn off the television, computer, radio, or anything that makes noise!

Probe and ask questions: You need to find out why she is upset. Don't speculate or assume that you know the cause.

1. Maintain an even voice tone.

2. Acknowledge there is a problem. "I can see you're upset. Do you want to talk about it? Is there something I have done?"

3. If she says yes, wait and listen.

4. If she says no, ask her to please explain why she is upset.

Empathize: Consider her perspective on the situation.

1. Look directly into her eyes and wait.

2. Listen to what she says without interruption.

3. Avoid being defensive in word and action.

3. If you are the problem, apologize... Oh, just apologize anyway!

Find a win/win solution. It will get you out of the doghouse!

1. Consider all possible ways to end the conflict. Come up with a plan to end the conflict.

2. *Both* of you need to agree on a solution. Physical touch is now a possibility.

3. Let there be Peace! (Making up is the best part!)

Learn from the experience. Maintain better communication in the future to avoid conflicts.

1. Sit down weekly to check "emotional balance."

2. Write down an agreement if necessary.

3. Verbally deal with it, agree not to allow this issue to be a problem in the future, and move on.

"The couple that laughs together stays together!"

Chapter 15

Your Place: What Do You Do Now?

15

Your Place: What Do You Do Now?

At some time or another in your life you will probably set up what was once called "housekeeping." It is a phrase that means you will have to purchase products, furniture, linens, kitchenware and so forth for use in your own apartment, condominium, or home. This is a simple list to help make this chore easy! Guys, this is not just for young guys setting up his first apartment. It is also for the single-again, starting over, male of the species. Listen up: Women do look at your place. You can no longer shrug your shoulders and say, "I am just a man," when excusing your living conditions.

Setting Up

Cleaning Products: Purchase glass cleaner, all-purpose cleaner, furniture polish, a room deodorizer, cleaning sponges, and cloths (not the same as the ones that you use on your dishes). You will need a liquid cleanser to use for cleaning tubs/showers and a toilet brush. Stock your bath with toilet paper (buy 6 rolls at a time), facial tissue, and a room deodorizer. In the kitchen, you will need paper towels (buy 6 rolls at a time), napkins, a broom, a mop, light bulbs, and dishwashing detergent. Purchase a broom and a vacuum cleaner for cleaning floors. For washing clothes you will need a bottle or box of laundry detergent and a box of dryer sheets. Also, don't forget to buy an iron and ironing board. (Yes, you will need them.)

Your living space will be addressed in four areas.

1. Living area (living room)
2. Kitchen
3. Bathroom
4. Bedroom

Area 1: Living Room

The seating area should include a sofa or futon and a couple of chairs, or a similar seating combination. Consider a neutral color scheme in selecting the upholstered furniture pieces. Black leather is not a good choice. Place a side table at each end of the longest seating area and place an appropriate lamp on each side table. When seated beside a lamp you should not be able to see the inside workings of the lamp. Place a coffee table in front of the sofa with some current reading material. Buy a stand or an armoire (tall wood cabinet) to house your television and sound/music system. Place one or two pieces of artwork or a single large mirror on the wall for decoration. When hanging artwork, the rule is to hang it at the eye level for a person of average height. It is always nice to have a clock in the room as well as a large candle or a couple of small ones to place on the side table. This gesture is an attempt at setting a romantic mood!

Area 2: Kitchen

Buy a four-place setting of china, a four-piece place setting of silverware, a set of good steak knives, a basic set of pots and pans, four matching water glasses, four matching wine glasses, a paring knife, a chef's knife, a middle-sized chopping knife, and a cutting board. You can buy four matching napkins and place mats, a corkscrew, a can opener, cooking utensils (such as a spatula, a large spoon, and a meat fork) and a colander (drains pasta), a cookie sheet, and two different sizes of casserole dishes with lids. Don't forget to purchase an oven mitt and a salad bowl set. Add these necessary items in your kitchen too: a trash can and liners, hand towels, and liquid hand soap.

Food for the kitchen

These items are necessities and should be kept in your cupboard or refrigerator at all times. Two or three boxes of assorted crackers, a couple of types of cheese, assorted soft drinks, bottled water, a bottle of red wine (room temperature), and a bottle of chilled white wine. Also, always have these food condiments available: salt, pepper, mustard, mayonnaise, steak sauce, barbecue sauce, hot sauce, and ketchup.

Area 3: Bathroom

Buy two (2) complete sets of matching towels, two bars of soap, a bottle of liquid hand soap to place beside the sink, as well as a nice set of hand guest towels. Buy a shower curtain with a liner, a bath mat, a toilet brush (in a nice container placed on the back side of the toilet), and a plunger (overflows are a hazard). In the cabinet underneath the sink, stock toilet paper and cleaning supplies. It is a good idea to keep on hand a couple of new toothbrushes for guests, mouthwash and toothpaste, as well as deodorant and some disposable razors.

Area 4: Bedroom

You will need a complete bed (a full mattress and frame), one bedside table, a good reading lamp, an alarm clock, a wood chest of drawers for folded clothing, two (2) dozen hangers, a hamper for soiled clothing, and a small wastebasket. Buy two (2) sets of sheets in a solid color (white is good), a mattress cover, a light blanket, a comforter or a bedspread, and two new bed pillows.

Visitors: How to Get Ready in 30 Minutes!

(You never thought they would visit, I know!)

Living Area: De-clutter surfaces, vacuum/sweep the floor; wipe off coffee table and end table surfaces; set out and light a candle or two, put on background music. Turn the light(s) on a low setting.

Kitchen: Clean off kitchen counters; clean the sink and table; sweep the floor; take out the garbage and put in a fresh garbage bag; check the refrigerator for drinks, and put away any dishes.

Bathroom: Scrub the bath, commode, and sink; wipe/mop the floor; put out guest towels; clean the mirror; deodorize the room; place a full roll of toilet paper on the toilet paper roller; close the shower curtain, remove soiled towels; close the toilet seat, and empty the trash can.

Bedroom: Hang up clothes; de-clutter all surfaces; and, make up the bed using clean sheets if time permits. Straighten the comforter; fluff pillows; put dirty clothes in hamper; turn one bedside light on low; spray deodorizer; and, vacuum/sweep the floor.

Collapse and enjoy the company of your visitors!

Chapter 16

Special Skills and We Don't Mean Karate!

16

Special Skills and We Don't Mean Karate! Take a Test.

Each person is born with natural abilities/talents and, in life, people add to these abilities through experience and training. Women are really attracted to men who exhibit some of these wonderful traits.

Look at the list below and check the ones that describe you best.

Athletic - is an active participant in sports.

Dancing - enjoys getting on the dance floor with his partner.

Massage - supports personal one-on-one relaxation techniques.

Writing - able to convey feelings into poetry or letters.

Volunteer work - denotes caring and consideration for others.

Organizational skills - shows an ability to plan and execute.

Well traveled - is well spoken and able to share experiences.

Public speaker - is comfortable in a public forum.

Musical - is able to convey feelings through sound (playing an instrument or singing).

Animal lover - shows he cares about small creatures.

Spiritual - shows a strong belief in a higher power.

Humorous - is able to entertain and make us laugh.

Good with hands - indicates he is good with tools.

Nature lover - shows a love of outdoors and history.

Artistic - denotes someone who is creative.

Charismatic - is charming, likeable, and powerful.

Scoring:

1 to 6	You are very talented and well liked.
7 to 12	Women are after you!
13 or more	Run for office!

Chapter 17

It's Over: Ending a Romance

17

It's Over: Ending a Romance

Some couples in an exclusive dating relationship at some time or another experience problems. Working out these situations can be difficult and emotionally draining. Sometimes you want to end a relationship and sometimes she does. The important part is to acknowledge it, discuss it, and then, if agreed, amicably walk away from each other. How you handle the end of a relationship will not only have a bearing on your emotions and those around you, but also on any future relationship(s) that you will have. Closure is very important.

Deal Breakers!

These activities *cannot be tolerated* in a healthy relationship.

Alcoholism
Drug Use
Physical and mental or emotional abuse of any kind
Sexual activity outside of the partnership
Criminal activity
Intentional and habitual lying

Acknowledge there is a problem.

1. Feelings have changed.

2. Habits have become irritants.

3. Being apart occurs more than being together.

Schedule time to discuss the relationship.

1. One-on-one, face-to-face time is critical.

2. Select a quiet area where there will be no interruptions.

3. Place a time frame on the discussion. (One hour is suggested.)

Rules of Conduct

1. Agree not to interrupt while the other is speaking.

2. Allow each person 10 minutes to present his or her side of the situation.

3. Emotional outbursts will immediately cause a 10-minute cool-down period for both people.

Listen and ask questions.

1. Consider the reason(s) the relationship is changing.

2. Allow each person to speak without interruption.

3. Be honest and sincere in stating your position.

4. Talk through your differences. Can they be worked out?

5. If the conversation becomes heated, take a break.

6. Determine if one or both of you want to save the relationship.

Save the Relationship

You *both* want to stay together.

1. Each person should state his or her needs within the relationship.

2. Come to terms with possible changes to make on *both* sides.

3. Agree to make every effort to honor your partner's requests.

4. If necessary, both agree to use a mediator/counselor to help facilitate a balanced, "healthy" relationship.

End the Relationship

You *both* want out of the relationship.

1. If living together, agree on a move-out plan.

2. Make a list of all personal items. Agree to a fair split.

3. Decide how to tell friends and family.

4. Part as friends and let the healing begin.

Chapter 18

Financial Balance: Money, Honey!

18

Financial Balance: Money, Honey!

People say most couples fight about two things, sex and money.

I will discuss only money here!

Money In: All income per year, including any and all sources.

Money Owed: Credit card balances, mortgage payment, car loan, and any personal loans owed to individuals or companies.

Fixed Monthly Expenses: This category includes mortgage/rent payments, monthly loan payments, credit card balances, utilities and insurance. Utilities will include electricity, water usage and phone. Insurance can include life, health, dental, and car, and homeowners or renters policies.

Variable Monthly Expenses: These expenses include clothing, repairs, maintenance, groceries, charities, gifts, vacations, Christmas, entertainment, and leisure activity cost.

Money for Short-term Savings: This category includes unexpected monies to go out, such as roof repair, car repair or an unexpected medical expense. This area is allocated for saving a down payment on a home, a car, or even a vacation savings. It is recommended that you always keep a 3-6 month normal spending amount to cover any and all emergencies. If possible secure this savings in an interest-bearing account that will allow you to withdraw money quickly. Replace any withdrawals as soon as possible to maintain this account for future needs.

Money for Long-term Investment: This money is for retirement. It is recommended that you save 10% of your gross income throughout your working career. How you invest it is determined by your age and your tolerance for risk. Long-term invested monies should not be removed except for a dire emergency.

Money Issues in a Relationship

1. Spending: People often have different spending priorities. It is not unusual that one partner is frugal (cheap) and the other is generous (overspends).

2. Saving: One saves money and the other doesn't.

3. Paying bills: One has good organizational and time skills and the other one pays bills late, if at all.

4. Personal Money: Each individual deserves some money to spend as she or he wishes without consent from the other.

5. Impulsive: "Buy now, pay later" is a fool's game.

6. Checking Accounts: His, hers, and/or a mutual account?

What is the best way to handle the money? What do you do?

1. Set up a mutual checking account to pay for all household expenses such as mortgage/rent, utilities (electrical, cable, water, and trash removal), entertainment and food. Decide on a minimum balance that must be maintained at all times in the account. Arrange for a safeguard such as a small savings account and/or credit card to cover possible overdrawn check charges. There is a hefty charge for having insufficient funds and it will ruin your credit rating to have checks "bounce."

2. Each person opens a separate checking account. This account allows

them to pay for their own personal expenses, such as personal health, life, and car insurance, entertainment, lunches, clothing, and child support.

3. Each partner commits a reasonable *monthly dollar amount* to be deposited in the short-term savings and another *monthly dollar amount* to be deposited in the long-term savings. Both names of the partners should be on these savings and/or investment accounts. Neither partner is allowed to withdraw any monies without the other partner's consent.

4. Decide on a maximum amount of money that either partner can spend without consulting the other partner. This spending comes from the mutual account for the couple. For example, you or your partner may want to pay the tab at a restaurant for some mutual friends, or one of you may find an incredible deal on an item that you both want. The amount allowed can be anywhere from $100 to $500, depending on your income level or money available. This arrangement allows for some flexibility when the other partner is not available for consultation.

5. Allow the most organized and "number savvy" partner to pay all of the monthly bills.

6. Set up and review a new budget every year.

7. Pay all credit card balances *off* every month. Pay on time to avoid late charges. Credit ratings are decided in a large part on *how well* you pay your bills. Keep one credit card for emergency use. This card will maintain your credit rating. Pay off and dispose of all other credit cards. Your final goal is to be debt-free!

Alternative "Box" Method

This *short-term system* may be utilized in the event you just cannot get the money situation straightened out! This is by far *not* the best way, but can be used for a short time. Select a container/box in a convenient location within the living quarters. Each partner deposits his or her receipt(s) for shared household expenses from where each has paid for an item or service. At the end of the month, all of the receipts are added and calculated. Expenses are to be equally shared, so the person that paid the least will make up the difference and pay the other person. I repeat: This method is not a long-term answer, and the box must be emptied on the last day of each month.

Chapter 19

What Does She Really Want? (Summary)

19

What Does She *Really* Want?

(Summary)

Traditionally people think of a gift as a material object given in a beautifully wrapped container or box. The truth is, a gift can be many things, because each person views gifts differently. Ask her which of these gifts are the most important and appealing to her. Which are the most important to you? Once you understand what she wants, the rest is easy.

For a woman, one of the best gifts is *language*. Women are very word driven and appreciate a man who speaks to them in honest, positive ways, including compliments, statements of encouragement, or praise for a well-done task/job. She loves to hear your voice directed to her alone.

A sense of *humor* is a wondrous thing! Laughter that spills out easily is joyful. This laughing signifies playfulness and an earlier time of happiness. She will always remember when you made her laugh!

Offer to do something without being asked! Ask her "What can I do for you?" For example, offer to run an errand, repair an appliance, or to plan/prepare a meal. A woman appreciates your *willingness* to help.

Affection is a physical way of communicating to her in a loving way. A hug, a touch on the arm, a kiss, or a time of intimacy is very important. Touch acknowledges that you care for her.

For many women the best gift is one of *time*. In this busy world it takes effort to step back and "make" time for you as a couple. She desires to spend private time with you alone and to have your undivided attention. Ask her out on dates regularly.

A *spiritual connection* with one another and a higher power strengthens a relationship. This creates a path that guides both of you to a mature life together.

Many material *gifts* need not be wrapped. The smallest object, whether it be a single flower, favorite candy bar, or an expensive item, can be equally treasured if the intent of the giver is to please the recipient. Surprise her with a small gift at unexpected times. Such a gift is a material confirmation to a woman that you are interested in her happiness. Ask her what gift(s) she wants. Give her what she wants, not what you want her to have.

Patience is a grand gift. Allowing her a safe place to speak, to be heard, and to be understood is priceless.

She wants to be a partner, not a passenger, with you. A future is a promise between the both of you. It is exciting, and speaks of adventure and plans of discovery. It may be as simple as going to a new restaurant, going on a trip, or planning a life together. It's about the *commitment*.

Good Luck, Gentlemen!

www.ingramcontent.com/pod-product-compliance
Ingram Content Group UK Ltd.
Pitfield, Milton Keynes, MK11 3LW, UK
UKHW041935190726
13854UKWH00004B/1606

9 781412 069496